What people are saying about Scott Butts

"For those of you who are police officers or military reading this, Scott Butts is one of the guys I wouldn't hesitate to go through a door with. Scott's ability to connect with people no matter what their background, skillset or intentions are is immeasurable. Whether he is teaching someone a new skill to help them reach their goals or sitting in a home with a broken family at 3 a.m. you can guarantee that what Scott is telling you is the truth. Not many people are as authentic and real as Scott is when it comes to helping others. In my opinion the world could use a few more people like Scott."
Rob House (G.I.S. Investigator, RCMP)

"Scott is a true leader in every aspect of life. He's excelled in work, friendship, love and sports. Scott has always led by example, and let's his actions speak louder than his words. This book is written by a true leader, a great example of taking responsibility for your actions and for your life."
Ryan Miles (West Jet)

"I have been a police officer for over 20 years and have spent a good portion of my career working with youth. Scott is a straight shooter and had a story. He was someone that had walked the walk and talked the talk. Scott Butts was such a valued addition to the team. I watched him transform lives before my eyes! He captivated the young minds and gave them the inspiration they needed to succeed! Scott has a true gift to lead, inspire and motivate. To this day, I still hear from students who tell me that Cst Butts changed their life."

Kathy Szoboticsanec (Lead Facilitator; Jean Minguy Youth Leadership Academy)

"I have never met an individual that is more committed to his word. When Scott says he will do something you can rely on the integrity of his word. That to me is one of the most precious gifts one can live as an example for our future youth leaders."

Fred Sarkari

Speaker – Best Selling Author

THE CONTINUOUS MOMENT OF YOU

You can Go Anywhere you want to,

If you know where you are

Scott Butts

www.ScottButts.com

Published by Zana Books

Copyright 2012 Scott Butts

Zana Books ISBN: 9-780988-1647-0-3

Visit ZanaBooks.com

Library and Archives Canada Cataloging in Publication

Butts, Scott
    The Continuous Moment Of You, You can Go Anywhere you want to, If you know where you are

Includes bibliographical references and Index.
ISBN: 9-780988-1647-0-3

1. Inspirational - Educational I. Title.

HD57.7.S37 2012   658.4'092   C2012-906179-9

Printed in Canada

Contents

ACKNOWLEDGEMENTS

I would like to thank all the people I have met over the span of my life that inspired me to write this book. Whether it was in my travels with hockey, my time spent on three University Campuses or in my work as a member of the Royal Canadian Mounted Police (RCMP). I have met many wonderful people who have shared with me without hesitation or concern.

I would like to thank the following people and families who were always there for me at every stage growing up, no questions asked:

- Chris, Devon, Heather and Brian Thomas
- Mark, Dennis and Kathy Simbirski
- Mike, Sean, Mark, and Maureen Podwysocki
- Garrett Everson for always treating me equally, never down playing my experience and always expecting big things from me.
- Ryan Miles for always being there for me for the last 18 years and helping me get to the next level.

To the following teachers who pushed and challenged me in several ways:

- Mr. TURNBULL in Grade 6 who taught me to respect myself with manners.
- Mrs. Arbuckle in Grade 7-9 who encouraged my boldness and guided me without hindering my learning and expression.
- Mrs. Machintyre in Grade 10 who challenged me to be more than just a Jock.
- Mr. O'Toole in Grade 11 who would not let me pigeon hole myself as just a hockey player and pushed me into the literary classics.

To my parents Robert and Carol who never stopped showing up to my hockey games despite how far away it was or how cold the night.

TO MY BEST FRIEND, Rina: What can I say about a woman who has single handedly guided me toward my dreams. You have never stopped believing in me and my vision for our family. Despite your request for privacy you never requested I not share this book with the world. You have grown so much as a woman and now a mother. It is an honor to watch. I will forever be in love with you. You always push us to grow as a couple. You are the best person to share a beer with and the best person to share my life with. I love you so much.

* * * * *

"There is so much more to the world than what you have experienced."

* * * * *

INTRODUCTION

It broke my heart to think of how this gritty but gifted 15-year-old boy was living. No kid should have to go through something like that.

I met Michael when I was 19-years-old attending Concordia University College in Edmonton, AB, working with high-risk youths. At the time, like most kids in care, there were limited spaces in group homes and many of them were being housed in hotels.

Some may think hotel living is not all bad; someone makes your bed in the morning, gives you fresh towels and cleans your room. But imagine living the life of an adult, alone, at 15-years-old. Michael's life was no vacation.

Michael grew up in an abusive, drug-ridden environment with very little support. He grew up watching his mother suffer a life of physical abuse, looked on as his friends became addicted to illegal drugs and saw his older brother go to jail. He was a tough kid but everyone had their breaking point.

One morning, without telling anyone, he decided he could not take it anymore. He had enough. Michael packed up his belongings and left. There had to be something better.

Winters in Edmonton can reach minus –40.6 °C (–41.1 °F) to –49.4 °C (–56.9 °F) and stay that way for weeks. Michael spent an entire winter on the streets. When I met him, he was badly in need of help.

I remember spending time in the hotel room with Michael talking about his life, where he was, and what he was trying to do. Michael was very specific. He wanted a job and a place of his own.

In an attempt to open him up to University life, I contacted my instructors at Concordia and requested that Michael attend a day of classes with me. They all unanimously voted yes and Michael and I were off to school.

It was early spring and the sun was shining as we excitedly made our way through campus to my philosophy class. Once inside, Michael immediately created a buzz. Everyone wanted to speak with him. During the lecture he even asked the professor a question of his own, "Who decides what is real?" His question prompted more class discussion and all I could do was smile; he was a hit.

"Who decides what is real?"

After school, as Michael and I were walking back to my car, we stopped at the edge of campus. As we turned to look back at the buildings, I noticed tears rolling down his cheeks. He was crying. Staring out at the reality he had just been a part of, Michael looked at me and said:

"I never knew this existed. I never knew that there was so much more to the world than what I have experienced."

We worked together a few more times after that, but eventually lost touch when I moved to Calgary; a few years later while in Edmonton, I ran into my old supervisor. She told me Michael was still receiving their help, was about to graduate high school and was looking into colleges to attend.

Your Life Is Your Story

All of your experiences and challenges, ups and downs, highs and lows are one continuous moment. We like to think of moments as something to steal, capture, and remember. We take pictures of moments, tell others about the time we saw someone famous and how we felt in the moment. But more than capture these moments, we must live these moments, connect with and learn from them.

"All of your experiences and challenges, ups and downs, highs and lows are one continuous moment."

The Continuous Moment of You is Your Story.

For some, their story is one of darkness and tragedy. For others it is a series of endless routines, hoping for special moments to come along. We long for moments where we feel alive. Moments where we can pull our shoulders back and stand tall with pride. But in between these moments we know something is still missing. We do not know exactly what it is, but we know we want more.

We go to concerts to feel something more. We work long hours to make more money. We go for a second helping at the buffet because we want more. We take on more projects, buy more stuff, and pay more bills. We are "more" addicts. We want more than just mediocre. We want more than just a few special moments. We want more out of life.

There is more to the world than what you have experienced. There is more to the story you have been telling. There is more waiting for you around the next corner, with your next handshake and in your next book. Just as it takes dozens of pictures to make a photo album, it takes a lifetime of moments to make a story.

"*There is more to the story you have been telling.*"

This book will change your story. This book will help you understand how to take the worst parts of your story and make them your best; how to turn your darkest times into your shining moments.

The Continuous Moment of You is the story of your life. It is the entire story, fact and fiction, your full make up. From the day you were born to the day you take your last breath. *The Continuous Moment of You* is your living biography.

"*From the day you were born to the day you take your last breath. The Continuous Moment of You is your living biography.*"

If you open yourself to the questions asked in this book and are honest with yourself, you will have a much clearer image of your current state and your future path. You will have a life-tested system to keep track of your physical, mental, emotional, spiritual, and financial health. You will have a better understanding of how to fix troubled relationships and how to take control of the choices you make. If you follow the system outlined, you will remain in the driver's seat of your life with a clear vision of the road ahead.

No one is perfect. Everyone has at least one thing in their life that needs improvement. There is a saying, "People don't know what they don't know." This book will help you find the answers to the questions you have yet to ask.

It did break my heart to think of Michael's life, his upbringing and what he went through. It breaks my heart to see people struggle with problems that are not their own. Throughout my hockey career, winning a National Championship, signing a pro-contract, and receiving an honorary Olympic Gold medal, I know what it takes to live a life of achievement. But every day as a police officer, I run across people, young and old full of unrealized potential. It breaks my heart to see people living small and I know it breaks yours.

We all know people in dead-end relationships with partners that only care about themselves. We all know people living pay check to pay check looking forward to the day they can retire only to receive a smaller pay check. We all know parents doing the best they can to raise their kids, who believe good parenting means sacrificing their own happiness and future for the sake of their kids.

When I was 19, there was so much more to the world than what I had experienced. When I was 19, I was fortunate enough to meet a 15-year-old boy that broke open not only my heart, but my mind. When I was 19, still a teenager, my heart would break yet again. This time for real, with not one, but two heart attacks in three months, entirely of my own doing.

CHAPTER ONE

* * * * *

*"No matter where you have been, where you are, or where you
are trying to go, you must know, **YOU** will always be there."*

S.B.

* * * * *

So Here You Are

Our entire life is made up of beginnings. We start a job, a new project or a new relationship. We often think of beginnings as a big deal. We celebrate birthdays, anniversaries, and have housewarmings. But when we focus on just one beginning, when they become singular celebrated moments in time, we lose connection with the little ones in between.

"Our entire life is made up of beginnings."

What about the day after you were born? Why do we not celebrate that day? What about the third month of your relationship? Is that not just as important as the first? Realistically, unless we want our lives to be full of endless party planning, we make big deals and celebrate only our significant beginnings. The day we took our first breath, our first day of school, or the day we join hands in marriage.

But beginnings are all around us. It is the beginning point from which everything after comes. The days in between your birthdays, the weeks in between Christmas and summer holidays, the breaths in between blinks, each have their own beginnings. In order for us to develop a clear picture of who and where we are at this point in our lives, we must break up our beginning points.

When we do this, when we break up and break down everything in our lives, we have a better idea of where we are. With a better understanding of where we are, we develop a deeper appreciation for the relationship between our continuous moments; between our past, present, and future. If we do not do this, if we do not develop a system for connecting our beginning points, we will not know where to start when we want to move forward. If you want to go to Omaha, Nebraska you must know where you are leaving from, as well as where you are going. But this is not the only thing.

Imagine competing in the track and field events of the World Games. You are a sprinter; one of the strongest and fastest athletes on the planet. Your event is the 100 meter dash. You are wearing your country's colors, waving to cheering fans, posing for pictures and getting warmed up for your time in the spotlight. You have run this race many times in practice and in competition. You know where it begins and where it ends. You know which lane you are running in. You know your fastest time and you know you will beat it today. As you loosen up, prepare yourself and get in "the zone," behind you, on the other side of the track, you hear a gun go off. Your stomach jumps up into your throat as you spin around to see what happened; it is then that you realize you missed your race.

You knew where the starting line and the finish line were, you knew your course of action and what you had to do when the time came. But to even have a chance at winning the race, you had to be in the starting blocks when the gun went off.

"But to even have a chance at winning the race, you had to be in the starting blocks when the gun went off."

It does not matter how fast you are, what matters is where you are at the start of the race.

You must start with where you are in order to know where you have been and where you are going. This gives you an image, a vision of your current situation and circumstance. Otherwise life is just a dash with no direction, no purpose, and no accomplishment.

"You must start with where you are in order to know where you have been and where you are going."

Originally, I thought I started this book when I was fourteen years old. This is not true. I have lived the process outlined in this book since I was fourteen; always sorting out paths, deciding on questions, and determining the most efficient course of action to reach my dreams. Just as your life is made up of many moments, so is the process of creating success in your life. Start living your truth now and it will get you to where you want to go.

Too many people say once they have their dream job, or car, or home, *then* they will be happy, then they will live that truth. It doesn't work this way. The road to success is far more enjoyable, beneficial, enlightening, and rewarding when you start living your truth now. This is your starting line. All the bumps and bruises along the way will help keep you on the path.

The focus must be on where you are right now. Not five years from now or five years ago, but where you are in this moment. You can start with your surroundings if you like. Right now I am sitting in my in-laws basement in front of a nice cozy fire two days before Christmas. You may be sitting in a bookstore, eating your lunch at school or at work, waiting at a bus stop, or working the night shift. Your next question could be anything, "How did I get here? Do I like where I am? How do I feel about the people around me?" Where am I mentally, physically, emotionally, spiritually and financially? What is most important is to ask and answer the next question.

The answer to your problems is in the questions you ask.

Leave no stone unturned. You must take everything into consideration. Everything that has ever happened to you, every major experience you have been through, all of the influences in your life; the way you were raised, the school you went to, the vacations you took or didn't take. Everything that shaped the current view you have of yourself and the world around you.

"You must be honest about your path and your choices in life."

You do not have to share these thoughts with others but you cannot lie to yourself. Why lie to yourself when you already know the truth? You must be honest about your path and your choices in life. You may not like or are proud of your journey thus far, but like it or not, the decisions you made years ago that you may regret now have made you exactly who you are today.

If you are bitter, then that is of your own doing. If you are lonely, then that is of your own doing. If you are sitting having pints with your best mate in a pub, then that is of your own doing. It does not matter how successful you become or how many goals you reach; your journey is what it is.

When you look at your life from this perspective, from the outside in, you develop a clearer picture of the whole. When you understand the importance of *where* you are in life, you can then go anywhere you can dream. You can still train, wave to the crowd and pose for pictures, but you will not miss the start of the race.

THE FOUR MOST POWERFUL WORDS I KNOW

The quickest and easiest way to knowing where you are is to stop, take a mental snapshot of your life and say to yourself, "*So here you are.*"

> ### " 'So here you are,' collects all of your experiences and brings them together in one moment."

"So here you are," collects all of your experiences and brings them together in one moment. It is like looking in the mirror and seeing not only your reflection, but a summary of the life that created that reflection. Don't look away for one second. Stay focused. If you are serious about this journey then look deep and hard at who you are right here, right now. With this phrase you continually force the truth out into the light even if the truth is ugly, overwhelming, or just too damn hard to admit. "So here you are" may sound like the end, but it is the beginning.

Throughout all of my triumphs and heartbreaks, this phrase, this mini life-assessment tool, "So here you are" is how I stayed focused and on track. They are four of the most powerful words I know.

When you know where you are, you have a starting point; a continuous point of reference. A roadmap to Los Angeles, California follows completely different routes if you are leaving from Seattle, Washington or Halifax, Nova Scotia. The power in the statement "So here you are," of coming back to the current moment and checking in is to make sure you are heading in the direction of your choosing; the right direction for you. "So here you are" is a pivotal point of the change process. It is like a wakeup call to your life every time you say it.

"So here you are." I wish I had a nickel for every time I uttered those words to myself. It did not matter where I was or what I was going through, whether it was a heart attack, my 13th hockey concussion, or sitting in philosophy class with a 15-year-old kid from the streets. I always ended up coming back to this point. This is where your choices, emotions, and experiences have led you. It is everything and absolute. It is the culmination of your life to date. It is not where you want or hope to go, it is *where you are*. If you do not commit to understanding where you are, everything that follows will not matter.

If you do not commit to understanding where you are, everything that follows will not matter.

We all want a beautiful home, a happy family, freedom to travel and loads of money in the bank. Our tendency is to focus on how we want to feel in the future, based on the dreams we have in the present. But focusing on future feelings and ignoring our present reality will always leave us wanting more. It is like catching water in a bucket with a hole in the bottom. It does not matter how much water we draw, the bucket will be empty when we go to use it. We can eventually own the fancy car and million-dollar house, but if we are focused on the product, we may never create the right foundation to support it continuance.

When you pass through a mountain tunnel, despite the darkness, you trust the road. You assume it will eventually end in daylight. Life functions in the same way. Everything before this moment you have already gone through. It is in the past. You are not stuck in it. Even if you are in the darkness of that tunnel right now, there is light on the other side. I have said for many years – if you are going through hell, keep on going. If you are *in* hell, you have not made a plan to get out of it. If you are *going* through it, you are moving toward the light.

The Continuous Moment of You is an ongoing dialogue, conversation, and relationship with you.

We have absolutely 100% NO SAY in what happens to us in our life.

Many authors will tell you that you control your fate, that you are the master of your domain, that you manifest your destiny, that you are the captain of your ship. These are only half truths.

While you may be captain of your ship, you do not control the flow or strength of the wind. You cannot influence the swell of the ocean or the direction of the lightning bolt. What you can control is your actions when the storm comes.

Picture this, an Army Major in a Prisoner of War (P.O.W.) camp sits locked inside a small, rodent-infested cage, and is tortured daily by soldiers for over five years. Every day pushed to the breaking point mentally, physically, emotionally and spiritually. This is the story of Major James Nesmeth. He *survived five years in a P.O.W. camp by visualizing himself playing rounds of golf* every day. Nesmeth realized he was going through hell, not stuck in it. He emerged from this experience stronger, smarter, and more dedicated to his life than ever.

So here you are. Do not take this lightly. This is an accomplishment. You are reading this book, have read, and will read others, trying to expand your mind and your experience. You want insights, secrets, tricks and tips; you are not satisfied with just getting by. Most people will never look this closely at their life and question it this deeply. They will never get to where you are right now. Change can be hard for some. Change can be scary. But change is not to be feared, it is to be welcomed. There is a lot more courage, pride, and resilience in you than you know.

As a police officer, I have seen and known people who have been through hell and would never dream of asking them to go through any of it again. But if they or anybody who has gone through what they have, does not process it or at least acknowledge their experience – including the role they played in it – they will always fall short of their goals.

Even some of our greatest entertainers, those who appeared to have reached their goals, achieve stardom, fame and fortunes were still battling their own inner demons; Kurt Cobain, Marilyn Monroe, even Earnest Hemingway. Outwardly successful, inwardly tortured. While selfishly, we may sometimes only want bad things to happen to bad people, bad things happen to good people all the time.

The Day I Learned My Greatest Lesson

I have never done anything half-assed. I thought once, that I had reached the peak of my goal, but I was wrong. No one willingly betrays themselves, but I did, unknowingly. I trained determinedly every morning, day, and night to get ahead. I set myself up for success, but was blindsided by circumstance. I sacrificed, put in more effort, and outworked my competitors, but life had a greater lesson for me to learn. One I was not prepared for and did not see coming. To this day, it was one of the greatest things to ever happen to me.

I worked tirelessly for five years trying to make up with effort, what I believed I lacked in talent. I vowed to myself that no one would work harder, pay more attention, and "show up" more than me. In my best efforts to improve, I forgot to appreciate what was already there. I ignored the scars I had collected and left wounds untreated. I was hurting and I didn't even know it.

I used illegal drugs to escape mental pain and convince myself I was more than where I came from. I consumed alcohol to numb my emotions, took pain killers to work through my physical pain and consumed steroids to grow muscular strength. I betrayed myself in my own best interests and pushed my body and heart to the point of literal eruption.

In the months following the heart attacks, the doctors explained to my family and I what had happened. A small piece of skin in my right ventricle was stopping the pulse from exiting my heart. I suffered from *ventricular tachycardia*, or "fast heart rate," and it was wreaking havoc throughout the rest of my body. The average person's resting heart rate is between 60 and 90 beats per minute. At the time of my second heart attack, my heart rate was 192 beats per minute for six hours. I knew I was lucky to be alive, but what I told myself was something completely different.

STEADY UP[1]! SHOW UP IN YOUR LIFE.

I may have been 19-years-old, but by not properly dealing with the scars, untreated wounds, and issues in my life, I created this experience. I allowed my darkest times and traumatic moments to define who I was. My heart was literally, the tipping point. From that moment on I began searching for the truth in my life. Absolute truth. Despite how hard and painful it was, I was going to push through and come out stronger on the other side. For me, there was only one way to deal with all of it: head on, full steam ahead, without prejudice. When you are in hell, keep on going.

"I allowed my darkest times and traumatic moments to define who I was."

These are the moments when we must rise above mediocrity. It is during your darkest times when you must shine your brightest light. It is during your toughest times when you must dig deeper and get tougher. It is in these moments that you take control of your life, learn from your experience, and never, ever look back. It is in these times that you must *show up*.

"These are the moments when we must rise above mediocrity."

---

1   During basic training with the RCMP, I assumed the role of "Right Marker." The Right Marker is the leader of a troop of new recruits and is in charge of making everything run smoothly. I would use the term "Steady Up" to gain the troops attention and get them to focus.

When you continue to "show up" in your life, especially when you need to most, you position yourself to be successful. It does not mean you *will* be successful, but at least you give yourself a chance to be. The rest is just effort and a few other important things I will discuss in the following chapters. Despite negative results, despite fears of the unknown, you have to keep showing up. If you are not willing to show up in your life, how do you expect to be able to succeed? If you do not ask yourself the tough questions, how do you expect to know the best answer? If you do not know where you are, how will you know where you are going?

Some believe there is a Higher Being that judges you. I have studied many religions of the world and all the great leaders, Jesus, Allah, and Buddha have essentially the same message; be true to yourself. Be honest with yourself and be accountable for your actions, but do not judge yourself negatively. True accountability is being constantly aware of what you are doing and not allowing anyone to distract or influence you negatively on your path. Without honesty and accountability, you will forever chase your dreams and never live them. Without honesty and accountability, everything you do from this day forward will crumble. Everything.

"Without honesty and accountability, you will forever chase your dreams and never live them."

No matter how motivated, excited, or dedicated you are about accomplishing a goal, you must know your position before the race starts. You must seek the truth regarding who you are and where you came from. Of course you can ask others for input. They can see things you cannot. But it is you that either accepts or denies their input and your truths.

We are all busy trying to succeed in our own worlds. Sometimes we can become so focused on our own point of view that we forget that others have theirs also. When we can see things from our perspective as well as others we will be much more appreciative of their journey and our own.

*   *   *   *   *

"I remember one day, standing on the overpass next to Concordia University College in Edmonton. Looking down at Wayne Gretzky Drive, I thought about how easy it would be to jump. The truth can be very scary and very real."

S.B.

I wasn't liked very much by some of the older kids in Junior High School. There were three grade nine boys that would beat me up before and after basketball and volleyball practice, every day, because I made them look bad in practice. I had more potential than they did *and* I outworked them. It pissed them off and they took it out on me whenever they could. Despite coming home with massive welts on my legs and being dunked in a toilet or locker almost daily, I showed up the next day for practice and worked even harder.

I came from a low-income household. Out of 65 kids at the Bantam AAA level, I was the only one who had a hand-me-down team jacket. The "poor coat" didn't even look the same as the new ones, but I wore it with pride. Every day, despite the ridicule, teasing, and the fights I wore it. I had a right to wear that jacket and I earned that right, every day.

When I moved up in the Bantam hockey league, it was no different. Again, there were three guys that had it out for me. After practice, when we took a shower they would piss on me and throw my clothes and hockey gear in the toilet. They would take my Maple leafs hat, shove it down the back of their pants, wipe their asses with it and throw it in my face. It was humiliating.

Early in life, I learned that no matter how bad it is, no matter the hell you think you are in, you *can* get through it. This was just one of the reasons why I decided to leave home for the first time at 15 years old and live on my own. I figured that if I managed to survive my home and school life up until that point, I could deal with anything.

"*I learned that no matter how bad it is, no matter the hell you think you are in, you* can *get through it.*"

For most of my early teen years I felt like I was in hell. I was being bullied every day at school by peers, older kids and my teammates. My parents were working their butts off to raise three teens, but there were always fights and arguments at home between us. I had a choice to make; I began living my truth and standing up for myself. I endured even more bullying at school and hockey because of this but I was not going to let others shape my life.

This was my life for seven years. Day in and day out, constantly looking over my shoulder, constantly wanting and striving for more, constantly trying to better myself. I was never the best player, but I was always aware of who I was, where I was, and what I was willing to do to reach my goals. I learned how to referee sports games to make extra money and be a better hockey player off the ice. I started to live the life I had imagined despite the pain. This was the foundation of my success later in life. No matter how hard things were at school, I fought back, kept my head up and moved forward with a clear picture of where I was going. No one dictated my life.

I remember when I returned to Calgary from being away playing Jr. "A" hockey. I would always run into the guys that use to bully me, piss on my ball cap, and throw my gear in the toilet. I would want to grab them by their now scrawny necks and punch them, but I never did. I had nothing to prove to them or anyone. Every time I ran into one of these guys I would always end up doing the same thing. Leaving the party when I was ready and never looking back.

Once you have learned from the past, leave it there.

In the end, after all was said and done, I was able to walk away from the game of hockey with my head held high. Out of these seven years, the one thing I am most proud of was my ability to always show up. Below is a list of times I showed up in my hockey career. Despite sometimes negative results I still triumphed.

- Cut from first Jr. "A" camp at the age of 16 (Concussion #2).
- Cut from second Jr. "A": camp at the age of 16 and sent to a Jr. "B" team.
- Worked hard for two months and signed with a Jr. "A" team (Concussion #3 & 4).
- Told the next year that I would have to try out for the team again; left because of verbal abuse from the coaches.

- Tried out and made the cut for another Jr. "A" team, was looked at for a scholarship to the USA but was cut because of team finances (Concussion #5).
- Tried out and made another Jr. "A" team and stayed the year (Concussion #6).
- Went to Boston and tried out for the United States Hockey League (USHL).
- Invited to Waterloo Blackhawks summer camp; lead the summer camp in scoring but did not make the team (Concussion #7).
- Tried out for the Vernon Vipers; cut the first skate.
- Joined another Jr. "A" team in Saskatchewan played great; did not sign with them.
- Join the Nanaimo Clippers and was cut after three weeks.
- Received a call from Waterloo of the USHL to come and play for them for the second half of the season. Coach was fired at the end of the year and the new coach told me I would have to try out again the following year.
- Signed with an agent out of New York.
- Signed a Pro-contract with the Anchorage Aces.
- Cut from the team after two months. (Concussion #8).
- Suffered my second heart attack while playing hockey in Montana.
- Underwent heart surgery to fix ablation problem.
- Played hockey for one year at Concordia University College (Concussion #9).
- Offered a scholarship at Lake Forest College, NCAA.
- Sustained a massive concussion (#10) that hospitalized me for two weeks.
- Underwent second heart surgery.

- Offered a walk-on tryout with Mount Royal University.
- First player in ten years to make the powerhouse program as a walk on. (Concussion #11, 12, 13.)
- Won a National Championship with Mount Royal.
- Two months later, retired from hockey as a player.

Think about the times you showed up in your life despite negative results. All of the times you took a shot and kept on coming, all of the times you took a beating and got back up, all of the times you made a bad decision and learned from it. Be proud of all the times you showed up in your life. If you did it once, ten times, or a hundred times, you can do it again.

"Be proud of all the times you showed up in your life."

"Why lie to yourself when you already know the truth." S.B.

NOTES

Your "STEADY UP!" Chapter Questions:
So Here You Are.

Where are you in your life as of right now in all of the areas outlined below?

1. Your Physical Health

2. Your Emotional Health

3. Your Financial Health

4. Your Mental Health

5. Your Personal Spiritual Practice

6. Your Career

7. Your Relationships

* * * * *

CHAPTER TWO

"Don't ever let somebody tell you... You can't do something.
Not even me. All right? You got a dream... You gotta protect
it. People can't do somethin' themselves, they wanna tell you,
you can't do it. If you want somethin', go get it. Period."

Christopher Gardner,
The Pursuit of Happiness.

* * * * *

Own Your Life

Do you have a pen or pencil, and highlighter in your hand? If not, could you please grab one? This is important. I would like to do a quick exercise with you. Once you have these items, could you please fill in the blank and then highlight it:

Write your Name Here

____

This is your book. By showing up on the page, you have confirmed your ownership of it. You can make as many marks in it as you want. You can write notes and reminders in the margins, underline sentences or quotes that stand out for you, and dog-ear pages if you want. If you have a coffee ring on the front cover it will still be your book. If you forget it in the lunchroom at work, it will still be your book. The next day when you go looking for it, it will still be yours whether you find it or not. If you value this book, you will take care of it and keep it safe. Because you own it, it is now your responsibility.

Owning your life follows the same principle. Ownership encourages us to take responsibility for our actions, possessions, and property. Ownership of your book, of your house, of your car, of your cell phone, of your identity all says the same thing: this is mine until I give it away.

By owning your life you are saying to those around you, 'Your life is yours, mine is mine.' No matter what they are going through, it is their experience, not yours. They can invite you into their experience or their drama, but it is you that declines or accepts the invitation. You can support someone but you do not have to take on their problems. Their sorrow is not your sorrow, their anger is not your anger, their depression is not your depression. This does not mean you are self-centered and heartless only caring for yourself. It means you can love and care for others without losing yourself. Owning your life means not letting outside influences or circumstances define who you are.

"You can support someone but you do not have to take on their problems. Their sorrow is not your sorrow, their anger is not your anger, their depression is not your depression."

When I was growing up, I was in such a panic to find my own identity that I unconsciously took on traits of others that I admired or believed to be "right". The summer I returned from living with two guys from New Jersey was hilarious. My family would laugh because no matter where I traveled I would return with a new accent and mannerisms. But to them, it made me seem less real and authentic.

Rather than claim ownership of someone else's traits, claim ownership of your uniqueness. Be yourself and trust the voice inside. Identify the values, beliefs, and patterns of behavior that you admire in others, mix them with your own and then choose what works best for you.

"Rather than claim ownership of someone else's traits, claim ownership of your uniqueness."

Many people feel they do not own their life because they are reliant on someone else, such as in a relationship. We hear the term "This is my better half," when someone introduces his or her spouse or partner. This suggests that without this person – their "better half" – they are incomplete. But since we should be complete before we started the relationship, how can we become incomplete within it? One of the famous lines from the movie *Jerry McGuire* captures this nonsense, "You complete me." This sentiment is not doing anyone any favors.

WHAT T-SHIRT ARE YOU WEARING?

People are the way they are. They can be nasty and nice. You do not have to take on their emotion as your own. Just because somebody is happy, does not mean you will be happy unless you allow yourself to be. On the flipside, if someone you deal with is mean to you, that may not have anything to do with you. Their anger or behavior is what they are wearing. My wife Rina refers to it this way, "That is their t-shirt, they have to wear it. That has nothing to do with you." Meaning, just because someone treats you with disrespect or hardship does not mean that you take on those emotions. If they are disrespectful, that is their t-shirt. You decide what you are going to feel, think, and do. You decide what t-shirt you want to wear.

> *"just because someone treats you with disrespect or hardship does not mean that you take on those emotions."*

Consider this. What if someone told you that you had the ability to filter every piece of information directed your way into something positive and rewarding? That no matter what happens to you in the future, you can re-frame the experience, re-channel it, and re-shape it into something more useable; something that helps you rather than hurts you. When you take ownership and full control of your life, this is possible.

Once you embrace everything, even the bad things, it will set you on a course for success that you cannot imagine. If you believe everything in your life is within your control, if you fully believe that you "own" every aspect of your life in complete totality, it is amazing what you can accomplish.

"Once you embrace everything, even the bad things, it will set you on a course for success that you cannot imagine."

Take a stand for yourself, show up in your life and take complete ownership of it.

No one likes to be micro-managed by another person. Having a boss or parent breathing down your neck trying to control your every move is suffocating. But you can micro-manage *your* life. This need not be an obsession, but make it your passion. You must seemingly go past the point of reason and take such control of your world that you no longer allow anything to negatively influence you. Once you have mastered this and as you evolve and start to apply these teachings, you can start to loosen the reins a bit and bring things back into balance. When you give your life to others you are out of balance. When you take it back, you reset the scales.

"So here you are" is where you are at this moment in every aspect of your life. It is a breakdown of everything that has happened to you and what has brought you to this point. It is the life lessons you received as a result of your challenges.

"Own your life" is the transition between what has happened to you, into being in total control of what you are going to do about it.

Once you understand that you are in control of your life, you become very selective in regards to whose opinion you trust and listen to. *Own your life* means you no longer give your personal power away to others or outside influences unless you decide to give it away. It means not giving others as much say in your life. It means you stop waiting for parents, bosses or bossy friends, or others to make your decisions for you. It means you **GROW UP**.

I tell street kids all the time, "No matter what you are going to do in your life, you must own your decisions." They must know and be aware of their plans and weigh the outcomes of each decision before they make it, especially the big ones.

> ***"No matter what you are going to do in your life,
> you must own your decisions."***

Owning your life is when you take full control of everything and from that moment on not let your past define your future. Your past can influence and educate your future, but it must not define it.

The Links between Ownership and Responsibility

Many children have a favorite stuffed animal, possibly a teddy bear or stuffed rabbit. They take it with them on road trips, they sleep with it at night, and are distressed when their stuffed animal is lost. Children understand early in life the value of ownership and most of the time, take responsibility for the safekeeping and care of their most valued property.

When you take ownership of your life and all parts of it, you appreciate the importance of taking better care of yourself. You take responsibility for your own safekeeping. You protect yourself when you are attacked, pick yourself up when you fall, and make better decisions because you have a vested interest in your property – your life.

> *"When you take ownership of your life and all parts of it, you appreciate the importance of taking better care of yourself."*

Once you truly appreciate the power of ownership and take responsibility *for* your choices, you then become more aware *of* your choices. Take happiness for example. Because you want to be happy, you make a choice to hang out with happy people more often. Because you recognize the value in hanging out with happy people more often, you feel happy when you are with them and praise yourself for making the choice (see Figure 1).

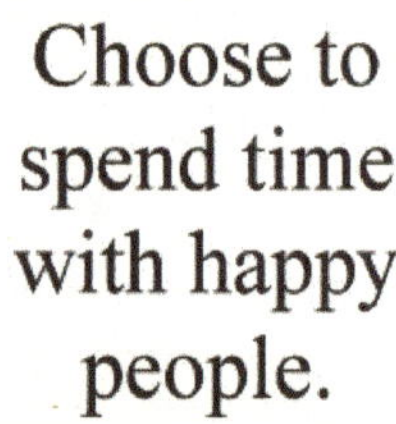

Choose to
spend time
with happy
people.

Praise
yourself for
your
decision.

Feel happy
when you
are with
them.

In this example you took *ownership* of your desire to be happy, and then made choices that supported your decision (hang out with happy people). If you wanted to feel happy, you would not hang out with miserable people. Ownership breeds responsibility.

The idea of "owning your life" is based on this premise. No matter what you encounter, do, or think, no matter how you act or react, you own the decisions, thoughts and feelings you have. When you take ownership of your decisions, thoughts, and feelings, you are less likely to make excuses or look for something or someone to blame. While we cannot always be in total control of what happens to us, we can, and must, be in control of what we *do* with what happens to us.

I remember sitting in rush hour traffic in Minneapolis, Minnesota with a friend of mine. With every start and stop of the car, she grew more and more frustrated. I turned up a song on the radio called "Shine" by Vanessa Amorosi in an attempt to emotionally distract her; no matter what we did or how we felt, we were still going to be stuck in traffic. Once we changed our attitude and point of view, we let go of the negativity of the situation and embraced the positive. It may have taken us an hour to get to home, but we enjoyed the rest of the drive singing and laughing all the way there.

Ownership means creating opportunities and then seizing them.

Our family had good friends who lived in Ontario. At the time, their son was playing in the National Hockey League for the Los Angeles Kings. When L.A. was in Calgary for the playoffs that year, I pulled the player aside and updated him on my hockey career. He said he would look into Jr. "A" and "B" teams in Ontario and let me know. Three months later I was on a Greyhound bus with all my personal belongings packed into a hockey bag. I had taken ownership of my life for the first time.

When I was 15-years-old, I was living in Calgary, AB with my parents and had just finished my second year of AAA Bantam hockey. On a bus ride back from a tournament in Abbotsford, I had a lengthy conversation with my coach. We discussed my future and where he believed I might fit into the picture the next year. From the conversation two things were clear: 1) I was a very talented player; 2) I was not going to be picked for the higher team. It had nothing to do with my talent, size, or personality. It was solely based on who I knew and who my parents were. Politics in sports; not the first or last time this has changed the outcomes of players' careers.

It was that spring that I made the decision to take control of my life and stop letting others have so much effect on it. The things that were out of my control, I would deal with. The things within my control, I would deal with. I was going to own my life and if anyone tried to interfere with my goals and dreams they would be met with fire.

"I made the decision to take control of my life and stop letting others have so much effect on it."

STEADY UP! TAKE CONTROL OF YOUR LIFE.

When I was a teenager, I was humbled by two heart attacks where I dropped to my knees, grabbing my left arm, gasping for breath in fear of my life. I could not control the fact that this happened. My "heart education" was what it was. What I could control was what I chose to do with this experience. I used it for motivation and a positive life change. There are no victims here.

You will not see someone successful put down another person who "failed" at the same thing, or anything. The successful person will encourage and respect the ones who keep trying because they know from experience that true success is just a few more failures away. In that sense, there are really no such things as failures; there are just success attempts in disguise.

In sports you see this kind of support all the time. The teams shake hands and offer respect to each other after the "battle" is over. Many times I would battle players on the ice over and over again always with the same ending; no matter who won, what remained was respect for each other and the offer of a cold beer. This is the side of sports that the public does not see and one of the sides I enjoyed most.

Ultimately it is your responsibility if you succeed or not. You have to ask yourself with every decision, "Is this moving me closer or further away from my goals and dreams?" When you own your life, you no longer pin blame or responsibility on others when things do not go the way you want. You stop leaning on others or using them as a scapegoat. In today's society, people have more crutches, excuses, and exit strategies than realistic plans, manageable goals and specific dreams. Should a plan fail or things not work out, they have an out before they are even in. They lack commitment. They are afraid of failure so they don't even try. To me, this is gutless.

"*Ultimately it is your responsibility if you succeed or not.*"

It Is Your Failures That Make You Amazing.

Music is a great influence in my life and to me, the band U2 embodies the idea of having a vision and staying true to the journey to get there. If you were to ask them, they might say that they are still on that journey and will be until their final days. Four musicians in an incredible band that continue to seek out their truth and share it with the world. Bono, the lead singer of U2, has been quoted several times, "*We do not make music for the rest of the world; we make music because that is what the four of us love to do.*"

I can say with complete certainty that if you want to succeed, get very comfortable with having absolute control over everything in your life. If someone labels you a control freak, so be it. Some will mock and make fun. They do not matter. They are motivation. The right people will appear and show up in your life. You are not looking to control others. Their life is their responsibility. That is the byproduct of owning your life; you become personally responsible for it.

In this process, it is important to trust the wisdom of your body and listen to what it is telling you about where you are and how you are feeling. It will tell you clearly what it most important in your life; pins and needles, shivers, and cold shudders are signs and signals that should not be ignored. When my heart was racing at 192 beats per minute, I was so in tune with my body I was able to tell the physicians my heart rate before they could.

Don't be a Lazy Thinker

"Mental laziness is one of the biggest poisons infecting our society today. "

Mental laziness is one of the biggest poisons infecting our society today. Simply because something is on television or in the news does not make it real. I wish we still lived in a time where media outlets could be trusted and were ethically conscious, but we do not. We accept information that is fed to us because we allow ourselves to think other people are more qualified to decide what information we need and don't need. Two people can look at the exact same thing and perceive it differently. We have a limited perspective. When we start asking questions we fill in the blanks. We get a better picture of the whole. Do your own research and question the ideas being sold to you. Own the information you are digesting. Take control of the intelligence you are putting into your brain.

"When we start asking questions we fill in the blanks."

How many times have we found out days or weeks after a media story broke that the information was misleading or not accurate? There are millions of people with wonderful advice for us; however, what is most important is how you interpret their message, and whether or not you accept their advice. We ultimately decide. Popular opinion is not on a compass; don't use it as your guide. Bruce Cockburn, a very talented musician put it this way, *"You have to kick at the darkness until it bleeds daylight."* Pink Floyd another one of my favorite bands put it this way, *"Did you exchange a walk on part in a war, for a lead role in a cage."* To me these lyrics are strong and clear. I would much rather be a soldier in my own war than a pawn in another's.

If and when you slip, forget about it and keep moving forward. It is not supposed to be easy; it is supposed to be work.

By owning your life you can avoid many bad habits that waste much of your valuable energy and time. Such as caring about things we do not care about. If it does not involve us or have any substantial connection to our lives, let it be. Some people follow every move of a celebrity like they were paparazzi. They boast that they know everything there is to know about a famous musician or actor from the sorted details of their personal lives to the type of toothpaste they use. Stop wasting your time wondering or worrying whose marriage is going to work out or not, or who is going to win *Survivor*. The life of a celebrity is no more important than your own. To suggest otherwise is an insult. You do not need your own life. If you remain dependent upon the approval of others for your motivation; you will run out of it. I often ask people who are feeling stuck, "Whose life is this?"

"As I walked into the sunlight, I came to realize that the world was at my mercy, and I the young dreamer, was free to live out my wildest fantasies on its stage."

S.B.

NOTES

Your "STEADY UP!" Chapter Questions:
Own Your Life

- What parts of your life would you like to change and / or improve?

- Are there parts of your life that you have given over to someone else to control?

- What do you stand to gain by taking back control of these things?

- What can you take responsibility for in your life that you have been blaming on others?

*   *   *   *   *

CHAPTER THREE

"Let me tell you something you already know. The world ain't all sunshine and rainbows. It's a very mean and nasty place and I don't care how tough you are it will beat you to your knees and keep you there permanently if you let it. You, me, or nobody is gonna hit as hard as life. But it ain't about how hard ya hit. It's about how hard you can get hit and keep moving forward. How much you can take and keep moving forward. That's how winning is done! Now if you know what you're worth then go out and get what you're worth. But ya gotta be willing to take the hits, and not pointing fingers saying you ain't where you wanna be because of him, or her, or anybody! Cowards do that and that ain't you! You're better than that!"

Rocky Balboa

*   *   *   *   *

KNOW YOUR WORTH

In 2011, I spoke at a leadership conference full of highly motivated 17 and 18-year-olds. To participate in the conference, the teens had to apply, complete exams and interviews, and undergo physical testing. This was the cream of the teen crop.

During one of the exercises I asked this question, "What do you expect from others?" They gathered in small groups, had ten minutes to come up with ideas and gathered three and a half pages of expectations for other people.

Then I asked them, "What do you expect from yourself?" With the same time and in the same groups, they were only able to come up with a page and a half of expectations for themselves. Even in a group of confident, competent and motivated young adults, their expectations of others were greater than they were for themselves.

My message to them was this. Holding others to high standards, does not mean we hold ourselves to the same ones. If we expect others to treat us with respect and kindness, we must expect the same from ourselves. When you expect people to act in a certain way, you are setting yourself up for either disappointment or hurt. Regardless of how others respond, if you take away the expectations you place on someone, you will be much more fulfilled in the end.

In the first few years as a police officer, I became so wrapped up with law enforcement that I forgot part of my job was simply helping others. Even people breaking laws and taking advantage of others need help. As a personal mission I began going out of my way to bring some of our local "clients" coffee and muffins for no reason. Not to make them like me, but to remind myself I had something to offer and could give to others without the expectation of receiving. I chose a profession where the expectation was to hold yourself to a high standard. If I was going to hold others accountable, I had to first start with myself.

It Is Time To Expect More From Ourselves, Rather Than More From Others.

What are your standards and expectations for you? Do you expect very little? Are you comfortable with a routine that is 'good enough for now?' Are you waiting for something great to happen to you financially in order for you to say you are worth something? Does a high income mean you have high worth?

I am convinced that if we were to hold ourselves to a higher standard, two things will happen: 1) we will be extremely successful, and 2) we will hold others to the same standard. How can we have expectations for others, without having the same for ourselves? When we define our worth, we position ourselves for success. At the core of every successful person's being is a tangible understanding of their worth or value.

The definition of "worth" is, *"The value of something measured by its qualities or by the esteem in which it is held."* With this definition though, who decides the measuring stick? Who decides which qualities to measure, what value to give them or even what a quality is? The problem is we spend too much time measuring our lives in comparison to people on magazine covers, in television, or on the news; people we do not know. It is all a matter of perspective. What is of value to me will not be of value to you. When you understand where you are in life and take ownership of it, you know that it is you that decides these things. You decide the qualities worth measuring and how to measure them based on your experience.

No one is more qualified at being you than you.

No one has a better understanding of what you have been through, what you have accomplished, or what you are capable of. No one has a better idea of who you are. No one has spent as much time with you as you. No one knows your worth more than you.

We are in relationship with ourselves every moment of every day. We communicate with ourselves, express our emotions, know our triggers and learn about ourselves every day. We know when we are sick and tired and when we are tired and sick.

As you read this chapter, forget that the word "worth" is usually associated with money and possessions and focus on your worth physically, emotionally, mentally, and spiritually. Are you worth being overweight? Right now I am ten pounds overweight and in essence, devaluing my worth. Some would say, "It's only 10 pounds Scott; it's not that big of a deal." But, it is to me. I would prefer to be 15 pounds lighter and very fit. That is of greater value to me.

Some people have overcome substantial physical odds to accomplish great things. These people were very aware of their physical worth. Even if your body has physical limitations, you can still work with what you have. Like him or not, to become the seven time, Tour de France Champion, Lance Armstrong underwent brain and testicular surgery to remove cancerous tumors from his body. Despite these terrible obstacles, no one but Armstrong knew what he was ultimately capable of and worth.

Mentally what are you worth? Are you worth a high school education or a Masters degree? Or is watching the house wives of Orange County of greater value to you? It is a matter of perspective and personal satisfaction. We decide the level of intelligence we are worth. No one has the right to say, "I am worth more than you." No one has the right to say attending a poetry reading at Oxford is better than watching *Ice Road Truckers*. You own your mental worth and your intelligence.

"Mentally what are you worth?"

Many people struggle with the fear of success. Are you worth success or are you worth talking down to yourself every day? Are you worth telling yourself you are too skinny, too fat, ugly, or worthless? Are you worth negative self-talk and self-sabotage or are you worth an uplifting personal message? Are you worth being bullied every day or staying in an abusive relationship or are you worth a healthy, positive environment? Even in deciding our own point of view, we are defining our worth.

How Do You Eat An Elephant?

One bite at a time. The greatest challenge with understanding your worth is when you realize there is a gap between where you are now and where you want to be. You will only set yourself up for failure if you define your worth as something completely unrealistic in comparison to your current situation.

For example, I have a day job, two sizeable mortgage, a 3-year-old child and another one on the way. I cannot just run off and write this book as if nothing else existed. I have responsibilities and other commitments. I have to be realistic. We have to consider our current and future worth based on our reality. If you feel you are worth a PhD in Astrophysics with 3% body fat but haven't finished high school and are obese, you have to be realistic; this is going to take some work. Not to say these measures of success are not attainable, but you must be prepared, willing to commit to the process, and see it through to the end no matter how long it takes. Always set yourself up for success.

Are you worth the effort it will take to reach your dreams?

I spent most of my teen years looking outward for value and worth. For many teens trying to find themselves, this is typical. Even at 35 years old, I am just now starting to feel comfortable in my own skin. I remember travelling from city to city, town to town, and team to team wondering if there was more to life than hockey. Amid my uncertainty, I started attending churches every Sunday morning looking for answers. I attended Christian, Catholic, Taoist, Buddhist, and Jewish services searching for something that made sense or spoke to me.

From Nanaimo, British Columbia, to Summerside, PEI, from Lake Forest, Illinois to Beaverton, Oregon, I spent five years in first-hand religious studies. They all seemed to share similar principles and there only a few certainties I came away with. What worked for me in the end was to take the best from all and adapt them to my life and personal spiritual practice. When I was in a very dark place in life, I was able to pull from all of these teachings and see my way through.

I spent a lot of years fighting to survive and fighting against what I did not want to become. All the while, I was fighting to get myself to a place where I could feel comfortable with who I was physically, mentally, emotionally, spiritually, and financially. Now, I have a very clear picture of what I am worth in these five areas. There will be times in my life when my worth will change, but now that I know how to handle this, I look forward to the process.

Keep in mind we live in a world where you must back up what you want. That is the beauty of our uniqueness and individual process. Each person must take responsibility for their worth. What works for one will not necessarily work for another. It is up to you to seek out the truths of your life. Choose what serves you best and discard the rest.

STEADY UP! JUSTIFY YOUR WORTH.

You will be the only one to suffer if you do not justify your worth. You have to be able to realistically reach your "worth goals" without losing balance of everything in your life. There has to be an evaluation of pros and cons when looking at each of them. If the cons far outweigh the pros, then you may need to re-examine what you want your worth to be.

"You must clearly define your worth"

There is no point sneaking around this subject. You must clearly *define* your worth. There are many mistakes that we make when it comes to what we believe we are worth or entitled to. Put your past experiences aside as a reason why you think you are worth something or not. Look at what you have earned and the situation you are currently in. The world does not care if you were abused, raped, forgotten, kicked, pushed down or left behind, they can only sympathize. All these events have earned you the right to learn from the situations, grow, and take from them what you want and then move on; keep moving forward.

While this may not seem fair, I can assure you that no matter what you have been through, someone else in the world has been through tougher times. We live in a tough world. Your challenges do not entitle you to what you believe you deserve. I have met a lot of people in my travels and the common theme among those that feel helpless and bitter is they believe the world owes them something. You will never succeed at life if you are waiting for the world to write you a check for the hardships you have been through.

"Your challenges do not entitle you to what you believe
you deserve."

You deserve one thing in life, life itself. That's it. People love to talk about what they think they are worth but are not willing to earn it. There is a big difference between thinking that you deserve, or are owed something and earning it. If we were all entitled to certain things, then every single human on earth would have them. In a fairytale everyone gets everything they want and treated the way they deserve but this is real life, not fantasy. We live in a world where not all people enjoy basic human rights or have access to food, shelter, clothing, and love. If you want something you have to work for it.

"You deserve one thing in life, life itself. That's it."

Define Your Worth

Defining your worth is a crucial step in the process of knowing your worth. In order to define your worth, you must carefully consider the following:

1. That which you believe you are worth…
2. Based on what you learned from your experiences, current training and education, and how you view yourself.

For example, in 2006, Christopher Gardner's climb to personal success was featured in both memoir and movie form, titled, *The Pursuit of Happiness*. In the movie, actor Will Smith played the lead role and his son, Jaden Smith played the role of Christopher Gardner's son, Chris Jr. As his story unfolds, through circumstance and choice, Christopher Sr. – who had custody and care of his son – found himself homeless, jobless, and broke.

Christopher Sr. went through horrible atrocities as a child including poverty, rape, and violence, but because *he believed he was worth more, based on what he learned from these experiences,* he kept on going. As an adult, Christopher was a medical equipment salesman but because *he believed he was worth more,* he entered an apprentice program in a stock brokerage firm *as he realized his limited training and education* would only get him so far. Through hard work and dedication he worked his way up in the firm and now owns a successful company.

By being honest with himself Christopher Gardner, took ownership of his decisions and *believed in his worth. Based on what he learned from his experiences, existing training and education and how he viewed himself,* he was able to realistically identify what he needed to do to succeed at the level he wished to reach. He increased his self worth because he felt justified in doing so; he had a good reason, the life of his son and himself.

If you find yourself in a position where you need to upgrade your education and skills, then go back to school, earn the credits you need and own your success. To improve our current situation, sometimes we have to take a few steps back. Too often people think it is too late to learn a new skill because they are too old or do not have enough time for more education. We have become so disillusioned in our society that we put value and worth on things that do not deserve it. When we put aside our ego and stop living in the world of instant gratification, we open ourselves up to new possibilities and new growth.

"We have become so disillusioned in our society that we put value and worth on things that do not deserve it."

Once you have figured out your worth physically, mentally, emotionally, spiritually and financially, then what? What do you do now? Simple, you get up, pack your lunch, go to work and you *earn your life*.

"When you know what you are truly worth, that is the moment when you are worth everything."

S.B.

NOTES

Your "STEADY UP!" Chapter Questions:
Know your Worth

1. Do you have any expectations for others that you do not have for yourself?

2. For you to increase your worth, what would have to happen?

3. Is there something you want in your life that with more education you could have?

4. What if anything, are you entitled to and why?

5. What barriers exist that keep you from realizing your worth?

CHAPTER FOUR

* * * * *

"The dictionary is the only place that success comes before work. Hard work is the price we must pay for success. I think you can accomplish anything if you're willing to pay the price."

Vince Lombardi

* * * * *

EARN YOUR LIFE

2001 changed my life.

I was playing hockey at Mount Royal University. We worked our butts off but success as a team seemed always just out of reach. There were guys sitting in the stands tracking statistics that used to lead their teams in scoring, they just wanted to be part of the overall success. They wanted to be part of something great. Finally, we got it together. Thirty guys decided to leave their egos at the door and no longer care about individual results and together, we won a National Championship.

The next year, on a high from the last, I went to the University of Calgary and was recruited to help train the Women's National Olympic Hockey Team. When I tell you that success breeds success, that when you are living your life the right people will show up at the right time, I am not kidding. When they won the Gold Medal at the Salt Lake City Olympics, because of my efforts and involvement with the team they awarded me with an honorary Olympic Gold Medal.

"you are living your life the right people will show up at the right time,"

If we give, and give only to receive,
then what we are to give,
will never be what we mean.

Having tasted excellence twice, I knew I could never look at life the same way. All of my hard work, everything I earned along the way, positioned me for success. From these experiences, I learned the value of team effort and of giving your best when you help others. If we took more time and helped others more, we could learn so much. If we got involved in what we believed in, rolled up our sleeves and went to work we would affect more lives than we could imagine. But sometimes, we are so stuck on a "return policy" for our efforts with others, that we miss what we are to learn.

If you earn something, you will learn something.

You can learn something by simply sitting and listening to a lecture, such as Michael and I did when we attending philosophy class at Concordia. But this does not mean we earned a degree.

Once we learn how to do something, we must put it into practice to earn the knowledge.

When I was accepted to the RCMP Depot Academy, I heard a lot of the same advice, "Put your head down, learn what you need to, and get out." However, I was not happy with just learning how to be a police officer, I wanted to earn it.

The "Right Marker" is the leader of a troop of 30 recruits and is in charge of making everything run smoothly for the entire six months of basic training. The number of times I was told *not* to be the "Right Marker" was astounding. If you meet any member of the Royal Canadian Mounted Police who held this honored position, they will tell you the commitments that came with it were unbelievable.

My 21½-hour day started at 05:00 a.m. and ended at 02:30 a.m. As a result of team effort and determination we were the first troop in three years to graduate all of our original 30 recruits. Yes, I am proud of this accomplishment and my role in our shared success but even with this experience under my belt, when I got to my first post in cold and rough, Terrace, BC, none of it made any difference. It was still get up every day, pack your lunch, go to work, and do your job.

Don't wait for it, work for it.

Any person who has done anything successful in any capacity will tell you that they have earned it. Tiger Woods in his early playing days is a great example of earning his success. While his talent is amazing, he won his tournaments and Championships by grinding out most courses during the week, positioning himself for success on the weekend. Most golfers will tell you while weekend tournaments cannot be won on Thursday and Friday, they can definitely be lost.

Abraham Lincoln spent over 28 years in politics. Over those years he endured 13 notable failures in his business, political, and personal life that would have emotionally crippled the average man. Lincoln knew his life worth and was committed to his goals; becoming the 16th President of the United States of America.

Everything so far is for not if you do not get up every morning, pack your lunch, go to work, and do your job. There is little point of spending time and effort in the previous three chapters if you say now, "Well that was fun but I do not want to work hard for it." As Fred Sarkari says, "95% of people get excited; the other successful 5% follow through."

Figure 2: Life Improvement Progression

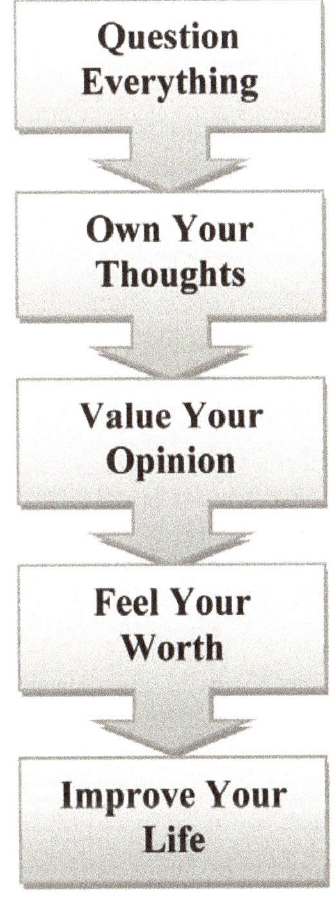

When you get up in the morning, pack your lunch, go to work, and do your job day after day, when you take full control of your life you have earned the right to question a few things. You make *informed* decisions. You take time to research things and evaluate the positives and negatives of any situation. If an idea is brought forward, you question its relevance and use in your life.

When you *question everything*, you take *ownership of your thoughts*. When you take ownership of your thoughts, you *value your opinion* and *feel the worth* in your life. When your life is worth something to you, you look for ways to *improve* it (see Figure 2: Life Improvement Progression). Improving your life is like earning your stripes in the military. It takes hard work, dedication and commitment.

"To earn your life requires work."

To earn your life requires work. You will have to work harder than ever before, but why wouldn't you? It is your life. Just like this book, you own it. Yes, things may get difficult, prior commitments may require your attention and outside influences may interfere. Some people are not comfortable with change; they want things to stay the way they are. Many times people will lie in wait and say, "Things are just not right yet," or "I am waiting for this to happen first before I make a move." If you keep working while you are learning, you will reach your goal more prepared and more aware. A journey of a thousand miles begins with one step.

"A journey of a thousand miles begins with one step."

What do you do when you reach the peak of a mountain?
Look for the next one to climb.

When I was 17-years-old, my goal was to get a NCAA hockey scholarship. I was going to High School, played Jr. "A" hockey and lived hours away from friends and family at my "billet's" residence. Your "billet" is the family Jr. "A" players stay with when they are away from home. To obtain a scholarship to an NCAA school, you are not allowed to accept money for playing hockey. The teams were allowed to pay your billet for living expenses but no money was to come to you directly. Because my parents were not able to fully support me, I had to support myself financially while playing hockey. Between school, hockey practice and a part-time job, my schedule was almost inhuman.

I was working the night shift at a trucking company so every morning I had to get up at 2:30 a.m. to unload tractor-trailers full of parcels for delivery that morning. After work, I went to school at 07:00 a.m., worked out, showered, ate breakfast, and went to classes until 3:30 p.m. After my last class, I went to hockey practice until 6:00 p.m. and then back to my billet's for dinner, did my homework and then went to bed at 10:00 p.m. When my alarm went off the next morning at 2:30 a.m., I would do it all over again. I can honestly tell you this was one of the most intense work schedules of my life. But I was committed to my goals and when you need money, it becomes very simple. You get up, pack your lunch, go to work, and do your job.

I did the same thing two years later in Waterloo, Iowa while playing in the United States Hockey League. Almost all of the guys I played with that year came from wealthy backgrounds and did not have to work, they could just play hockey. Not me. I had to wake up every morning at 02:00 a.m. but this time instead of unloading trucks, I worked with three other guys to remove snow from the streets of Waterloo's downtown core. Trust me when I tell you, it was hard work. Spend one winter in Northern Iowa and you will know what I am talking about.

I did not tell you these two stories to impress or gain your sympathy. I had no clue what I was doing when I packed up all my belongings, hopped onto a bus and travelled across Canada to go play hockey. What I did know however was where I wanted to go, what my goal was, and what I had to do in order to reach it. All of my activities including the jobs were what I had to do in order to achieve that goal. It really is just as simple as that. Once you clearly define your worth and the goal you are trying to accomplish, there is but one thing left to do; earn it.

"Once you clearly define your worth and the goal you are trying to accomplish, there is but one thing left to do; earn it."

STEADY UP! Deal with it.

Do you have a minor injury or ailment? If it is not life-threatening, deal with it. If it is life-threatening, deal with it. Don't let it stop you from reaching your goals and living your life. Your injury or condition is your circumstance, not your life. We all seem so fragile and so sensitive. If you were abused as a kid, I get that. But what do you want, an apology? While you're waiting for your apology your life is passing you by. Ask Oprah Winfrey if she is still looking for someone to apologize to her about the hell she grew up in.

Deal with the things you need to deal with and let's get going. Sitting on your ass accomplishes nothing but growing a bigger ass. If you have not dealt with things from 5, 10 or 20 years ago, you are just scared and lazy. You decided that what happened to you has defined you. You have the strength to deal with those things. You are worth more than that but you have to believe it for yourself. I can only tell you what worked for me; you have to figure out what works for you.

One of the things I talk about in presentations is, "Peak the day you die." Since we do not know when we are going to die, you must climb your mountain every day. I know many people who still live in the past, still live their high school championship as if it was yesterday, or speak of college as the best years of their life. If you have decided that you no longer need to grow, learn, adapt, or evolve, then hand in your life card and get out of the way of the rest of us.

"'Peak the day you die.' Since we do not know when we are going to die, you must climb your mountain every day."

Your Life Is A Privilege, Not A Right.

After you are born, every day you have on this earth is a privilege. It is a privilege when you live in a country where there are no car bombings on every street corner and suicide bombers on our buses. If you want to squander your freedom and complain about how bad it is or how tough you have it, that is your choice and from my perspective, a poor one. If you are not motivated and excited about your life yet, now is the time to take action. Once you have a clear understanding of what it is you want, the hard part is over and the fun begins.

"Once you have a clear understanding of what it is you want, the hard part is over and the fun begins."

Some call me outspoken, bold and loud. Some who have known me have seen the fiery side of my passion. I do not work hard to impress others. I work hard for my own personal satisfaction knowing I have earned my life.

"I work hard for my own personal satisfaction knowing I have earned my life."

We are not preparing our young adults adequately enough. Students are leaving college or university believing they are entitled to a job. Just because you have an education does not mean you have earned anything else. They are surprised that they have to work for the job they really want. All a university does is teach a specific topic and tell students when to show up for the class and the exam. The rest is up to them. Knowing there are people not willing to invest 2, 3, or 4 years of their life and reap the benefits for the next 40 baffles me. Invest in yourself, your skills and your future; it pays off every time. The minute we stop believing the world owes us something is the minute we take our lives back.

People buy lottery tickets, hoping and praying for $1 million, thinking it will change everything. But what does $1 million *really* do? It is no coincidence that most millionaire lottery winners go bankrupt within five years after winning their jackpots. The problem with winning the lottery is the money was not earned and because it was not earned, the winners do not know what to do with it when they have it. They blow it and end up back in the same place they were before they won, or worse.

Work hard and smart. We read books about working smart and not wasting your energy. But what we do not realize is when we work hard and smart, we get ahead that much quicker. When you work hard, you learn something. Then, the next time you work hard, you have that much more to work with. It is a balanced cycle.

USE THE 1 ½ RULE.

Those trying to gain a competitive advantage, whether in business or sports, use the 1-½ rule. If your competition trains two hours a day, then you train for three. If they do everything at 100%, then you do everything at 150%. Whatever your opponent or competition is doing, you do the same amount, plus half. This is why runners train at high altitudes and why swimmers train with clothing that produces more drag. They make their training harder using the 1 ½ rule and increase their performance.

> *"If your competition trains two hours a day, then you train for three. If they do everything at 100%, then you do everything at 150%."*

One of this country's greatest hockey talents was Wayne Gretzky. For Gretzky to accomplish what he did – being only 6'0" and 170 pounds playing in a sport full of grizzly men – he needed to use both effort and intelligence. He was able to see the ice and the game in ways no one else could. He worked harder than most people. His level of commitment was untouchable.

I agree everyone has the right life, but from the moment you get your feet under you, you must earn everything. You earn your grades, you earn your pay, and you earn your success. Satisfaction comes with the exhaustion you feel after a long day's work knowing you laid everything on the line and left nothing on the field. Yes, we must love what we do, but it is how hard and how well we do it, that provides us the most satisfaction.

Whether you get out of bed or not, your life goes on. You can invest in yourself or sit back, grow old and wonder, "What if?" Don't spend time trying to convince yourself that things are not the way they are. Don't wait for the end of your life to look back and realize you didn't live up to your highest potential. Earn your rewards. Earn your congratulations. Earn your applause.

After 7 years of being a police officer, the most gratifying part of my job is after my last night shift, when the clock hits 6:00 a.m. When I walk out of the police station and head toward my truck I feel the calm of the city. When I envision people sleeping safe in their homes I feel a sense of pride. I am not unrealistic, I know bad things will still happen. My pride comes from knowing I did my job.

Whether you are flipping burgers or delivering papers, be the best burger flipper and the best paper thrower anyone has ever seen and take pride in your work. No matter what your beliefs, upbringing or personal history, there will come a point when you will have to do things for yourself. Your life is your responsibility. By earning your life and allowing others to earn theirs, you ensure your success. Good enough is never ever enough when it comes to being successful. *"There is so much more than good enough."* Sara McLachlan.

"Good enough is never ever enough
when it comes to being successful."

"Those that say do not do. Those that do, do not say."
Unknown

NOTES

Your "STEADY UP!" Chapter Questions:
Earn Your Life

Write down 3 goals and after each one, write one sentence that captures what you will have to do with each one in order to earn the outcome you want?

1. Goal #1:_______________________________________

    I will achieve this by:

    ____

    ____

2. Goal #2:_______________________________________

    I will achieve this by:

    ____

    ____

3. Goal #1:_______________________________________

    I will achieve this by:

    ____

    ____

CHAPTER FIVE

*   *   *   *   *

*"You find out life's this game of inches, so is football. Because in either game – life or football – the margin for error is so small. I mean, one half a step too late or too early and you don't quite make it. One half second too slow, too fast and you don't quite catch it. The inches we need are everywhere around us. They're in every break of the game, every minute, every second. On this team we fight for that inch. On this team we tear ourselves and everyone else around us to pieces for that inch. We claw with our fingernails for that inch. Because we know when add up all those inches, that's gonna make the difference between winning and losing! Between living and dying! I'll tell you this, in any fight it's the guy whose willing to die whose gonna win that inch. And I know, if I'm gonna have any life anymore it's because I'm still willing to fight and die for that inch, **because that's what living is, the six inches in front of your face.**"*

Al Pacino (*Any Given Sunday*)

*   *   *   *   *

COMMIT TO YOUR JOURNEY

A plane that takes off from New York to L.A. is off course 80% of the time. They use intelligence to adjust their heading, but they are always moving forward to the destination they have committed to. Once you understand the principles outlined in this book (see below), it is your level of commitment that will see you through.

1. *So here you are*: your mini self-assessment tool to help you evaluate all aspects of your life and situate yourself on your own timeline.
2. *Own your life*: Take responsibility and control of your life.
3. *Know your worth*: Define and justify your own worth and personal value.
4. *Earn your life*: Work for what you want, and make your life your passion.
5. *Commit to your journey*: Stick with your plan and vision and follow though.

Here is an example of how the above principles played out in my life.

When I moved out of my parents' home at 15 years old, I knew exactly where I was and the truth about my life (*so here you are*). On a three-day bus trip to Northern Ontario, I decided I would never again allow anyone but myself to have control over my life. From that moment on, I owned everything (*own your life*). Each time my skate hit the ice I worked hard. In every classroom, at every night job and during summer training, I worked hard. I knew my talents and personality and had a reason to succeed (*know your worth*). I earned every opportunity I encountered. I was not the best player on the team but vowed to be the hardest working one (*earn your life*). Yes, there were kinks to be worked out, re-adjustments to make, roadblocks and negative influences to overcome, but I vowed to keep going (*commit to your journey*).

One day, it all came to a head and I saw the light at the end of one of my greatest tunnels.

After spending three years bouncing around Jr. "A" leagues in Canada and the United States, I signed a pro-contract with the Anchorage Aces in the West Coast Hockey League. I had reached one of my original hockey goals, to play professional hockey. It was an amazing feeling but it was short lived. I was not ready.

It was a difficult pill to swallow but that is the essence of commitment. For me, there was no other option but to keep on going and try again. After healing from my first heart surgery, more moves and signings around Canada and the U.S., more concussions, and another heart surgery, I returned to Canada and finished up my hockey career at Mount Royal University where we won the National Championship.

"For me, there was no other option but to keep on going and try again."

I know you have a story of triumph too. I know you have a goal that you have always wanted to achieve. I know you are the type of person that can make it happen. You made a commitment to yourself when you opened this book to read it. With each chapter you confirmed your commitment. With each word you processed and digested its messages. I know you will be successful because I know you are committed to your success.

"I know you have a story of triumph too."

I promise you, you will never look at life the same way again.

Once you have realized your true potential, life takes on a whole new meaning. Your beliefs, passions and excitement will guide you and fuel your journey, but it is your commitment to the process that matters most. Only you can decide what level of commitment you are willing to give to any goal. Without commitment your goal is simply an idea. Commitment is what takes you from "A" to "Z."

"Once you have realized your true potential, life takes on a whole new meaning."

Like anything else you have to be committed to a goal in order to achieve it. The difference between people who enjoy moderate success and people who experience excellence is they never lose sight of the end result and stay committed to the process.

You can show up to the race, be ready in the starting blocks for when the gun goes off, but if you want to win the 100 meter dash, you have to run 101, 102, 110 meters. Stopping at 99 meters is not enough. You must commit to greater than 100 meters to have a chance at winning.

Just as the definition of success is different for everyone, so too is the definition of commitment. Commitment means you are willing to see your goals through to the end knowing there may be sacrifices to make. It means once you have decided you want to do something, you do exactly what is required of you to carry it out. No matter the obstacles in front of you or the difficulty of the challenge, success involves staying focused and on course.

In the big picture, it's the little things that count.

Recently we renovated our basement. I did the tile work, the framing, the drywall, the plumbing, the electrical, and the painting. It looked amazing and I felt proud of my accomplishments. However, out of all of the tasks I completed, what gave me the most trouble was the length of the spout for the bathtub. It did not matter how great everything else looked, the smallest thing gave me the greatest grief. I had to go back to Home Depot three times to get it right.

Neglecting the little things in our projects and lives, have the same effect. They can come back to haunt you and give you the most stress. We must commit to following through with all of the little things as they are important pieces of the overall picture. If you neglect details and tasks in a project, even a single item, the foundation will be poorly laid and the entire project or plan will eventually crumble.

"We must commit to following through with all of the little things"

Every decision you make, no matter how small or great creates your life. No one knows the thoughts you have, the ideas you don't share at meetings, or the way you feel about things, even the little things. You are in constant communication with yourself. You know you best. From the kind of coffee you drink, to the faith you believe in, to the person you are going to marry.

"Every decision you make, no matter how small or great creates your life."

This May Not Happen Overnight

You decide your timeline and your progress. Success can take days, months and years but if you are committed to your goals and make them a realistic priority, you will get there. Once you fully understand the power of commitment and its ability to fuel your journey, your momentum grows. Smaller commitments will change over time, but the big ones will keep you going. Right now, my wife and I are balancing two professions, moved a 104-year-old house, and manage a growing family. When you understand the value of commitment, it becomes easier to decide which goals to commit to.

Commitment is often seen as a romantic word with little appreciation and understanding of its meaning. Everyone has dreams of success, but few achieve that success. The trouble lies in the strength of their commitment. People can get excited about a dream but few follow through. They see the level of commitment required to see it through to the end, but get frustrated and stop.

Working the streets as a police officer for 7 years, I continually see the level of commitment in someone with a drug addiction. As odd as this may sound, it takes commitment to be addicted to cocaine, crack or any other drug. Whether it is through theft or robbery, they are committed to finding the means to obtain money for their drug habit. They are committed to finding the drug and the people who have it. Most of them truly feel they will die if they do not get it. Addicts will go to amazing lengths to get their next high.

The word commitment is very close to the word addictive.

Everything must be in balance. Sometimes people can go so far over the top that they become unhealthy and develop and addictive mindset in achieving their goal. For example, if a person's goal is to have the most extensive coin collection in the country, they are making a commitment to the process of becoming a coin collector. If their interests grow to the point where their relationships suffer, they have lost connection with balance. The strength of their commitment has turned the goal into an obsession. Keep in mind, our objective is to reach our goals and enjoy the process and challenge in reaching them. There has to be a balance between your commitment and your reality.

I had a commitment to succeed in hockey. When I was 15 to 18-years-old my friends would come home for the summer. We would go to parties almost four nights a week, but before I went and hung out with them, I would go the gym, get in my two hour workout and then join the group. Just because my friends wanted me to go to the party early did not mean I had to. A balanced commitment to success meant it was okay to go to the gym *and* have a good time with my friends in the same evening.

> *"Do what you have to, so you can do what you want to."*
> **The Debaters.**

Commitments must be strong enough to bend but not break. There will be times when you will be pulled off your path. You will get sidetracked, stalled, or stuck altogether. Life happens; things will get in the way. Commitment means no matter the delay or diversion, you always come back to your goal.

In hockey, I learned if I wanted to improve, I would have to play with players who were better than me. In life, the same happens. If you surround yourself with people who are positive and excel, you will bring your game up. When we live our lives to the highest level, we bring others up around us. If you surround yourself with negative people that continually drain you, you will underperform. The poem "Our Deepest Fear", by Marianne Williamson states this exactly;

Our deepest fear is not that we are inadequate.
Our deepest fear is that we are powerful beyond measure.
It is our light, not our darkness that most frightens us.
We ask ourselves, who am I to be brilliant, gorgeous, talented,
fabulous?
Actually who am I not to be?
Your playing small does not serve the world.
There's nothing enlightened about shrinking so that other people
won't feel insecure around you.
We were all meant to shine, as children do.
It is not just in some of us, it is in everyone.
And as we let our own light shine, we unconsciously give other people
permission to do the same.
As we're liberated from our own fear, our presence automatically
liberates others.

You must strongly believe in what you are doing, commit to see your way through, and use an eyes-wide-open approach. An eyes-wide-open approach means you do your research and know exactly what is expected of you to see your goal through to the end. Unloading trucks or shoveling snow at 3 a.m. was not my idea of teenage fun, but I was committed to my success so I did it. When in doubt, use the "1-to-5" rule: what you do today, will affect you five years from now.

What is your big dream?

On his 24th birthday, Rudy Ruettiger decided he did not want to work at the town steel mill anymore. He was committed to his life dream of playing football for the University of Notre Dame Fighting Irish. He went to Community College to pull up his grades, worked with the grounds and maintenance crew at the University and slept in a storage room at the field. He lived like this for two years until he was finally admitted to school.

Once a student, Rudy set his sights on making the football team and tried out as a walk on. The problem was at 5'6" and 165 pounds, Rudy was an undersized football player. Despite what he had to overcome, he made the practice squad but not first string. Every day he gave his best and worked hard in practice. While he was living his dream, he had yet to reach his ultimate goal, to play in a game as one of the Fighting Irish. When the coaches told him he was never going to get a chance to play in a real game, each one of the starting players offered their spot for him. They saw and recognized his commitment not only to the team but to his goal.

Rudy played in two plays, recorded one quarterback sack, and to this day is one of only two players to ever be carried off the field in celebration. His, is an amazing story of commitment and perseverance.

STEADY UP! MAKE UP YOUR MIND.

Commitment means, "No matter what." If not today, when? We are going to wake up tomorrow and be 60 or 70 or 80 years old. I am not sure what the hold-up is? Start making plans and stop making excuses. If you are committed to your goal, it will not matter where your starting point is. If you are waiting until everything is perfect to start, you never will. Fight for your inch. Claw for it. It is what makes the difference between living and dying.

"Commitment means, 'No matter what.'"

Even the process of writing this book started the same way; I was never quite ready. I worked on it for 19 years but never thought I had enough information to start. I did not think I had enough credibility. I wanted to help, motivate and inspire people to succeed but I did not know how to bring it all together. Then I started working with Fred Sarkari and he helped me fill in the blanks and gave me the tools I needed to make this work.

You may not have the answers but you have the means to find the answers. Start, and start today. Nobody has all the answers at the beginning of a journey but once you get started, you will spiral in the right direction. It takes 21 days to form a habit. The more days you put off starting the longer it will take.

"Nobody has all the answers at the beginning of a journey"

Sometimes the greatest thing that can happen to us is to be humbled. Being knocked on your ass can be a wonderful thing. All you do is get up and learn from it, ask questions, seek advice, and look outward to people who can assist you. I love not knowing the answer to something. I know the journey will reveal the answers to me.

Succeeding is not a hard thing to do.
Just make up your mind and get it done.

A stubborn man with vision and passion for his life started what we now know as Kentucky Fried Chicken. Unsatisfied with his poor social security payments, Colonel Saunders set out to sell his chicken recipe. He was told "NO" 1009 times before someone said "YES" and agreed to sell his recipe. How many of us would quit after 100 or 500 "NO's"?

You must have clarity when everyone around you is either not on board or opposed to your goal – clarity in chaos. There are no quick fixes. Either you are in or you are not. You have to decide your level of commitment when people around you are saying that it can never be done and never be accomplished. They are just pushing their lack of commitment onto you. This may take years. Years you have. Second, third and forth chances you have. Time you have. Those that love you will support your effort. When you can stand in the middle of a crashing thunder and lightning storm and still hear your own voice, that is commitment.

Lifelong commitment is this; you have a goal, you reach it, you start another goal. The moment you succeed is the same moment you start working toward the next goal. There is no break; there is no stopping and smelling the roses. People who are truly successful know when to enjoy their success, but if you were to ask anyone who is successful, they will tell you that they are always working toward the next goal.

Success Is Following Through

Showing up will only get you part of the way there. You have to follow through and see everything to the end to be successful. No matter how long, how difficult or how stressful the journey, you must follow through.

When I look at my life and see how far I have come, I am grateful. From being abused as a kid, bullied in my early teens, lost and depressed as a late teen, two heart attacks, heart surgery and 13 concussions in my youth, to where I am now is NOT a success to me. Not allowing these challenges to define me IS the success to me. Not allowing my challenges define me is a success. I will peak when I die, until then, I will push through.

The only thing I would separate from my success accomplishments would be my relationship with my wife and love. We have been together for ten years now. Coming together is a beginning, working together is progress, staying together and pushing forward is my greatest success.

"Commitment is making your goal a priority in the midst of your current reality."

S.B.

NOTES

Your STEAD UP! Chapter Question:
Commit to your Journey

Choose one of the goals you identified at the end of Chapter 4: *Earn Your Life*. With this goal, *write down in detail your exact plan to carry it out* and see it through to completion. Try to be as detailed as possible when you do this.

DEDICATION

This book is dedicated to anyone who has ever looked at his or her current place in life and wanted something more. To anyone who knew exactly where they were in their life and how they came to be there. To anyone who woke up on this day and decided they were not happy with their current view of themselves and their life.

This book is dedicated to anyone who has spent most of their life putting others first hoping that someone would do the same for them and realizing it is them that puts themselves first. To anyone who is ready to stand tall, take full responsibility for their life, know where they want to go and need a little help getting there. This book is dedicated to the dreamer, the star gazer, the believer and the romantic who wants something so much more than good enough.

This book is for anyone who is sitting on the verge of greatness and nervous to take the next step. To anyone who has experienced some success in their life and wants to replicate it. To anyone who stands so close to the top of the mountain that they can imagine what the view looks like. This book is dedicated to the scared, to the brave, to the unselfish hero who lives every day awake and alive. To anyone who has ever seen someone else do something that they have always admired, knew they were capable of, but did not know where to start.

This book is dedicated to the down trodden, the helpless, the bullied, the beaten, the scared, the abused, and the forgotten. To anyone who has ever been told "no", that they were not good enough, not tall enough, not strong enough, not rich enough, not smart enough, or not brave enough. This book is dedicated to anyone who has seen the road to hell and gone through it. To anyone who began a journey because they believed in themselves, only to be tripped by someone else before the finish line.

This book is dedicated to YOU. To all and every part of YOU. This book is dedicated to YOU standing up, holding your head high, seeing where you want to go, knowing how to get there and then never, ever stopping for the rest of your life.

STEADY UP! GO FOR IT!

THE CONTINUOUS MOMENT OF YOU

www.ScottButts.com